Are you ready to have fun?

THOMAS FLINTHAM'S
BOOK OF
MAZES & PUZZLES

D1390118

For Dad.

www.thomasflintham.com

Welcome to Thomas Flintham's Marvellous Mazes! All kinds of super-amazing maze adventures await you inside the pages of this book. I hope you have lots of fun. Don't get lost!

Hello! We are the maze technicians. We're experts on everything there is to know about mazes.

We are going to fill you in on everything you need to know to solve the mazes in this book. Don't worry, it's all really simple.

A

B

Every maze has an 'A' symbol and a 'B' symbol, and the aim of every maze is to get from the 'A' to the 'B'.

Each maze has a 'B' symbol, like this. This is the point in the maze you need to try to get to. When you have found your way to the 'B' symbol, you've solved the maze!

The 'A' symbol marks where each maze starts. No matter what the maze looks like, you always start wherever the 'A' symbol is.

There are many different kinds of mazes in this book, and they don't all look the same. Don't worry, though, there is an easy way to see how each maze works.

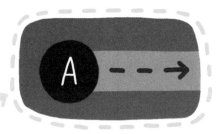

At the start of every maze, there is an arrow coming from the 'A' symbol. This arrow shows you where to start your route and is the key to understanding how each maze works. By looking at the arrow and where it goes, you can figure out which parts of the picture make up the maze.

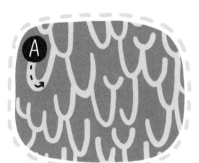

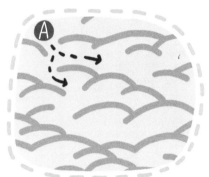

Here are some examples of the different kinds of mazes. See how the arrow shows you the way each maze works?

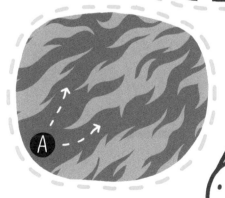

That should be all you need to know to solve the mazes. Some mazes are harder than others, so if you get stuck on a tricky one, why not leave it, try another one and come back to it later? Good luck, and have fun!

Welcome to Mazeland!

While you are here you will see wonderful sights and have some amazing adventures. Here is just a taste of what you have to look forward to:

No matter where you go in Mazeland there is always someone interesting to meet. The maze people all have one thing in common — they love solving mazes!

Keep an eye out for Astro Pete, Mazeland's number-one astronaut. You wouldn't believe the amazing things he's seen while exploring outer space!

Mazeland is full of heroes, just like the Little Knight, ready to take on its many adventures. He might be small, but he can easily deal with Mazeland's biggest challenges.

They're in the woods. They're even up the highest mountains. Mazeland is full of all sorts of animals, creatures and critters. How many will you see?

B

The one thing you'll find in Mazeland, no matter where you go, is mazes! They're everywhere! Hard ones and easy ones. Long ones and short ones. All kinds of mazes in all kinds of places! Please enjoy your visit to Mazeland. We hope that you enjoy seeing all the sights and solving all the mazes!

Turn the page to start your maze adventure!

Let's begin!

The wolf howls in frustration at the moon and its tricky maze. No matter how hard he tries, he just can't solve it.

Did you know that deer like to play hide-and-seek with each other? Well, they do!

(Don't forget you can jump from the antlers to the branches.)

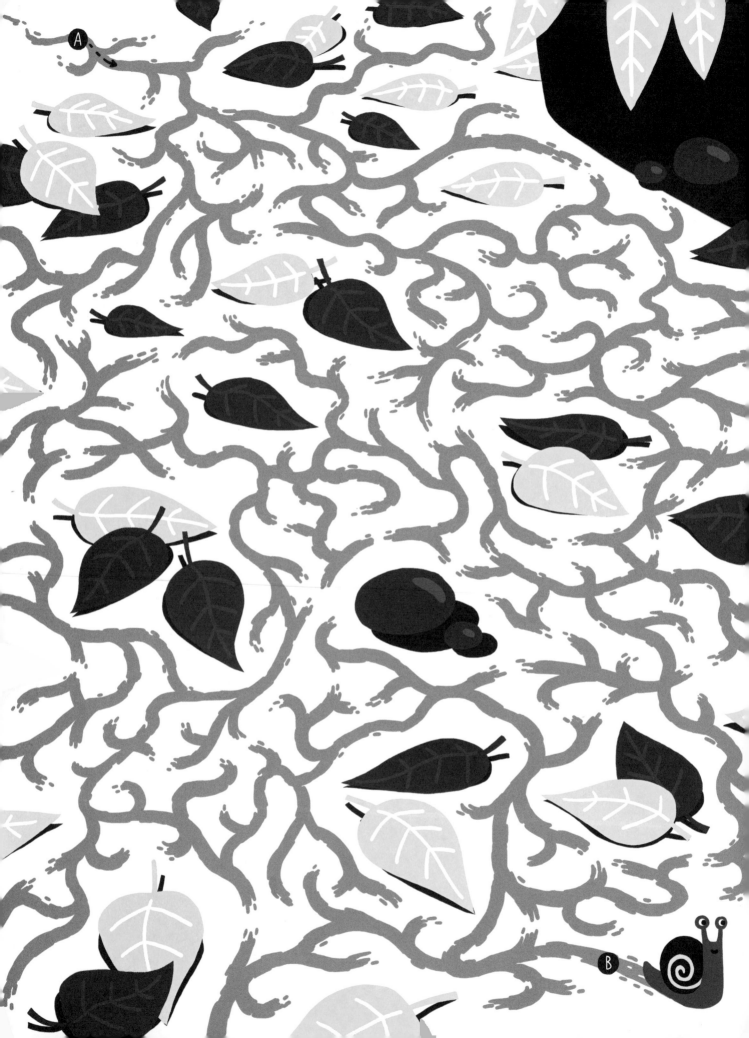

THE LITTLE KNIGHT
AND THE CURSED CROWN

One day the prince came to the Little Knight to ask for help with a royal emergency. The king had been turned into a monster!

A wizard had given the king the gift of a shiny new crown, but it was a trick! As soon as the king put on the crown, he was transformed into a scary, hairy beast!

The prince fled the castle in fear. He knew the only person who could save the king and get the castle back from the wizard was the super-brave Little Knight.

The prince gave the Little Knight a map to the king's island, and without delay the land's smallest adventurer set out to save the day!

With a swing of his sword, the Little Knight chopped the wizard's magic wand in half, freeing himself and taking away the wizard's magic powers.

The now powerless wizard was captured and locked away inside the King's prison.

The cursed crown was locked away where it could do no more harm.

"Thank you so much, Little Knight," said the King. "If it wasn't for you, I'd still be a monster and the wizard would have taken over my whole kingdom. I can't thank you enough, little guy."

The Little Knight wasn't really listening though. He was busy thinking about how terrific his shield would look with a maze painted on it. Don't be rude, Little Knight!

The End

Bethany's favourite pictures at the art gallery are the classical portraits. She thinks this one is beautiful.

Ramona loves all the modern art at the gallery. She likes trying to figure out what each painting is about. This painting is called 'Scattered Well'. What could it mean?

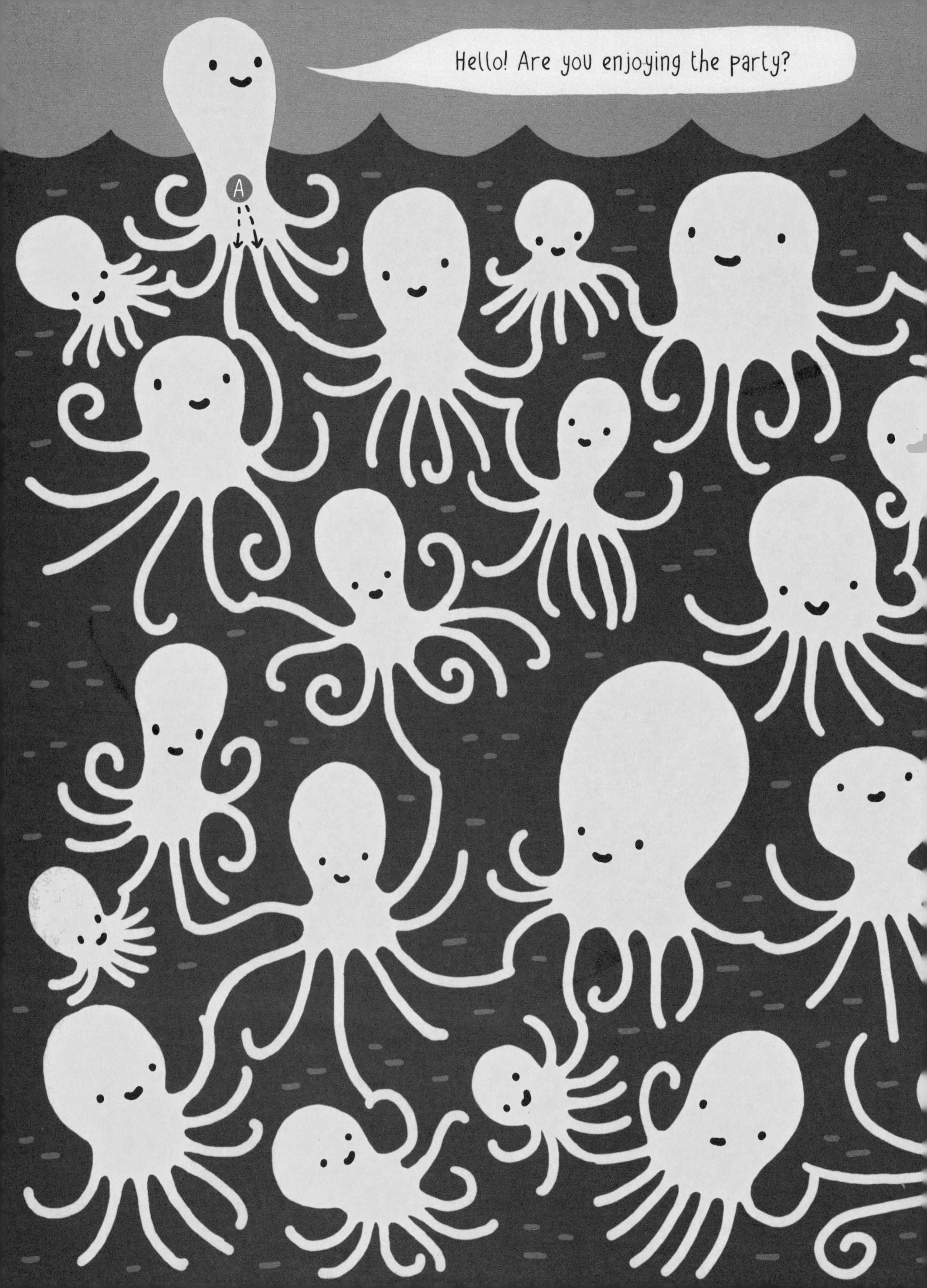
Hello! Are you enjoying the party?
A

The spider was too busy playing and lost track of time, and now he's late for his dinner. He'd better get back home quickly or Momma-Spider will be mad.

What do dogs dream about when they sleep?

THE ADVENTURES OF Astro Pete

THE PERFECT PLANET PROBLEM

Meet Astro Pete, legendary astronaut and space explorer. After many years of space adventures he has decided it's time to find a planet to make his home. Surely the perfect planet can't be too hard to find. . .

Astro Pete had only just settled in to his new house on the Planet Dagnog when he decided it wasn't the right planet for him. Although it was very nice in general, the main problem was that it was covered in giant astronaut-eating super-monsters! If he can get back to his Super-Amazing Rocket without being eaten, he's sure that the next planet will be perfect.

The Beedax
(Likes chasing astronauts, catching astronauts and eating astronauts.)

Astro Pete's House
(Completely monster-proof. Well, hopefully...)

Ⓐ

The Broodal
(Has four smashing, bashing fists, ideal for smashing and bashing yummy astronauts.)

The Vigon
(Has a super-big eye to help it find astronauts to eat.)

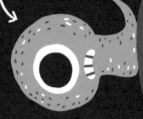

The Glongfob
(A kind of ghost that doesn't understand why all the other monsters eat astronauts when it's much more fun to just absorb them.)

The Bortbort
(Has lots of teeth to crunch astronauts with.)

Ⓑ

The Blibnag
(A big, moody monster with a very bad temper, super sharp horns, and an endless appetite for astronauts.)

Planet Dagnog's moon
(The various craters and shadows on the moon look like a scary face!)

Astro Pete's Super-Amazing Rocket
(Totally monster-proof.)

Before he can get to the next planet, Astro Pete has to carefully get past the super-hot flames of a nearby sun. Be careful, Astro Pete, those flames are very, very, very hot!

The Planet Wist is hot. Very, very, very hot in fact. Far too hot for poor Astro Pete. After ten minutes on the planet he feels like he's about to melt! He'd better stick to the shadows and get back to his rocket before he becomes a barbecued astronaut!

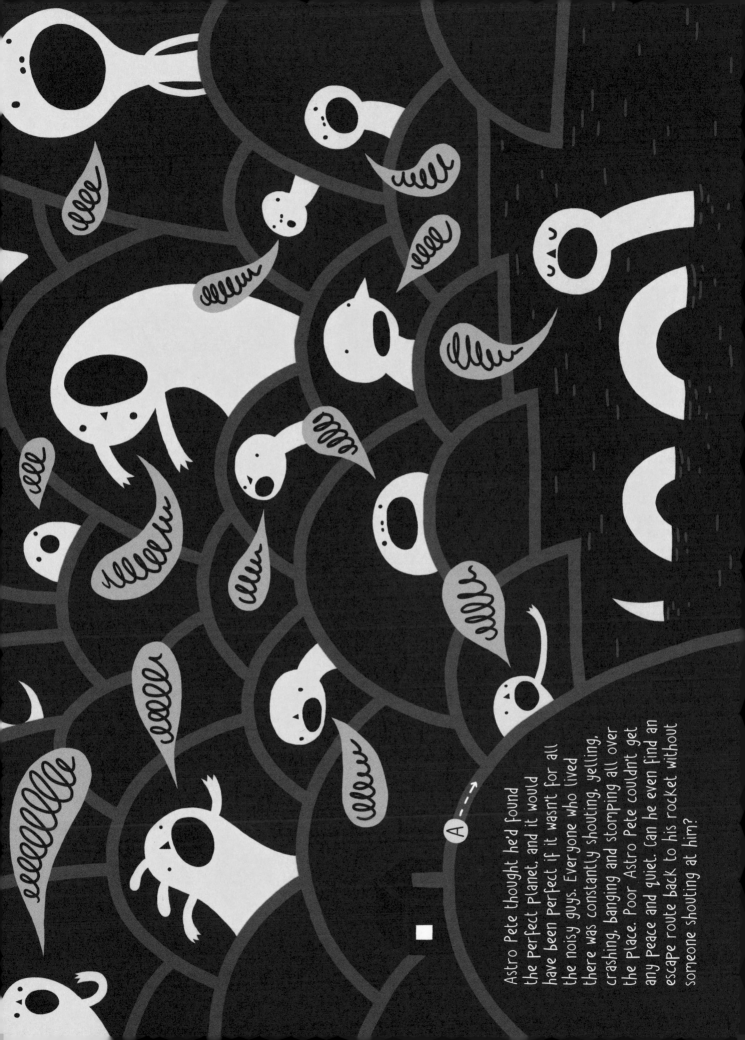

Astro Pete thought he'd found the perfect planet, and it would have been perfect if it wasn't for all the noisy guys. Everyone who lived there was constantly shouting, yelling, crashing, banging and stomping all over the place. Poor Astro Pete couldn't get any peace and quiet. Can he even find an escape route back to his rocket without someone shouting at him?

Astro Pete's been sucked into a wormhole! If he can make it through, he'll find himself in a completely different part of space with new planets to try. If he can make it out, that is...

The Planet Bixxo is just too small. Don't give UP Astro Pete, surely the next planet will be better.

Astro Pete (A normal-sized guy, not a giant despite how it might look.)

Planet Bixxo's moon (Also small)

Astro Pete's Space Boots (size 8)

A

B

Flowers (Not trees)

Space snail (Same size as a normal snail.)

As Astro Pete approaches another planet, he is hopeful that this time he has found the perfect place to live. Is this the new home he has been looking for all this time? There is only one way for him to find out, and that is to land and have a good look around. Good luck, Astro Pete!

The Planet Sneep is a very crowded place. The whole planet is covered in super-tall skyscrapers and massive, endless crowds of people. Within a week of living there, Astro Pete was fed up of being constantly overcrowded and surrounded all the time, with no open space on the whole planet where he could take a break from it all. He decided it was time to make his way through the crowds, back to his rocket to continue his search. Poor Astro Pete.

After a long and unsuccessful search, Astro Pete found himself back where he had started on the Planet Bib.

After his adventures, Planet Bib seemed very different. It was still very dull, but that didn't seem so bad anymore.

It wasn't too scary.

It wasn't too hot.

It wasn't too loud.

And it wasn't too crowded.

Astro Pete decided that Planet Bib wasn't a bad place to live after all. Yes, it was a little dull, but that was what made it the perfect place for him to rest in between his many exciting space adventures. Astro Pete loves to return home for a little break, with nothing else to do but relax and solve some of the moon's mazes. He's found the perfect home at last!

The End

Fox in the snow, where will you go to find something nice to eat? Why not have a look in that bin?

The mouse needs to get back to his mouse hole without being seen by the hungry owl. He should probably stay in the shadows to be safe.

A field full of hungry crows is not a nice place for a little worm to live. If the worm could make it to the scarecrow, he should be safe from harm. Watch out for those crows!

Far, far away
in the deepest forest
at the top of the tallest
trees, sits king Wishing-bird.
If you find him and tap his
magic crown, he will grant you
any wish you ask, as long as you
ask very nicely
and feed him a lot
of chocolate.

Daniel has an imaginary friend called Mr. Huss. Mr. Huss is very good at hide-and-seek and storytelling, and likes to help Daniel solve mazes. When they work together there is no maze they can't beat!

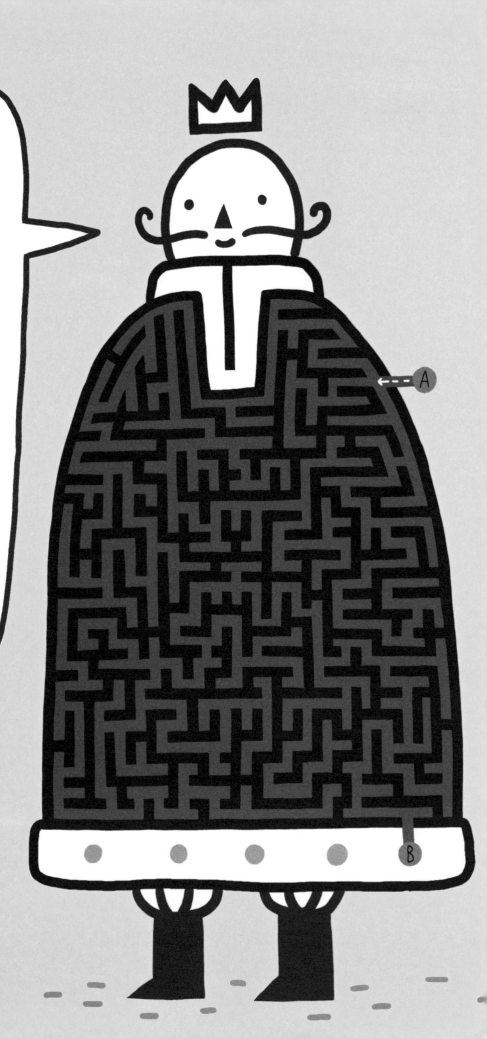

Welcome to Puzzleland!

We hope you enjoy your visit to Puzzleland, where you never know what puzzling place, person or creature you'll find next. Wherever you go, and whoever you meet, the one thing you can certainly count on is that you'll always find a puzzle to solve. Here is a quick look at what you'll see as you adventure your way through the always puzzling Puzzleland!

Keep an eye out for all the different kinds of animals in Puzzleland. How many can you find?

With all the puzzles that need solving in Puzzleland, it's a good thing there are lots of robots to help out.

The early bird catches the worm, but which worm has it caught?

Alice is always being bothered by a giant invisible cat. Why won't it leave her alone? Can you see it?

The dogs are having fun playing fetch in the sea. It is very busy though, and sometimes it's hard for the dogs to find their balls. Can you help each dog find the ball it's looking for?

IMAGINARY
FIG

MONSTER
HT!

Jim is fishing for fish, but the lake is so full of rubbish he might have better luck catching an old boot! There is one fish for him to catch though. Can you help him find it?

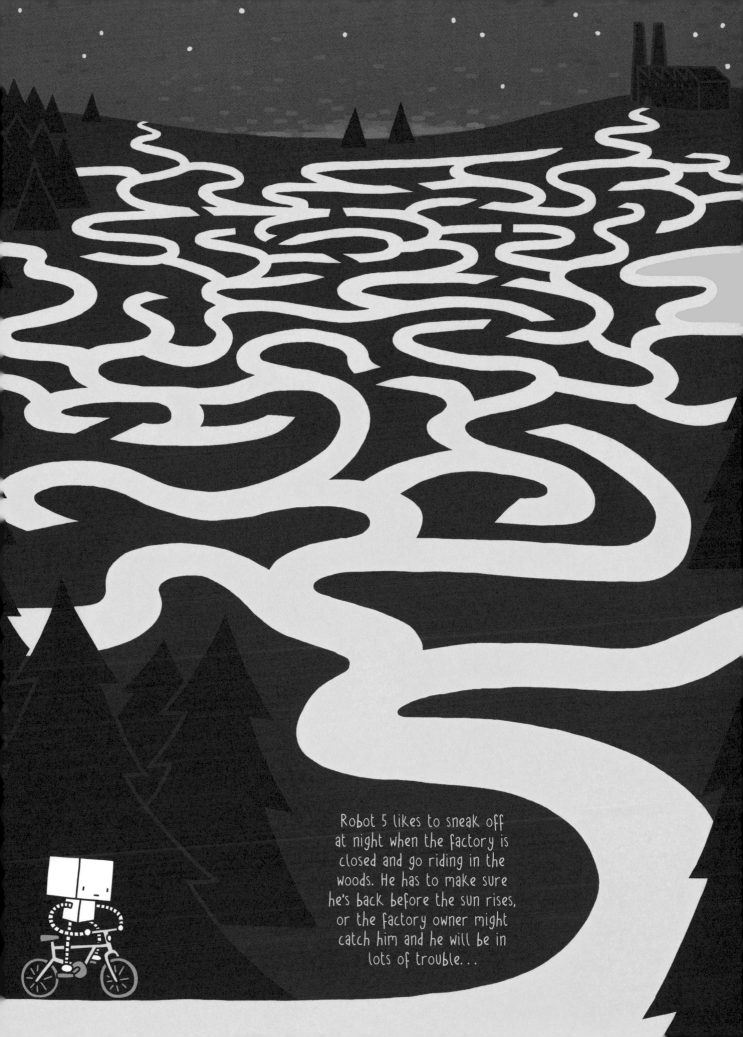

Robot 5 likes to sneak off
at night when the factory is
closed and go riding in the
woods. He has to make sure
he's back before the sun rises,
or the factory owner might
catch him and he will be in
lots of trouble...

Once a month all the twins in town meet up for a thorough discussion of all twin-based issues and for a nice chat. The main draw is really the many delicious cakes provided by the Baker twins. This month, without anyone noticing, someone without a twin has snuck in to the meeting so that they can help themselves to the cakes. Can you spot the lone intruder?

The bull has escaped! Quick! Who's caught it with a well-aimed lasso?

The children are picking rare mushrooms for their uncle. He gave them a list of markings that normal mushrooms have. Rare mushrooms don't have any of the markings mentioned on the list. Can you help them find 5 rare mushrooms?

MUSHROOMS WITH ANY OF THESE MARKINGS ARE NOT RARE MUSHROOMS:

1. Black zigzags

2. A sad face

3. Black or grey triangles

4. Grey spots

5. Black horizontal stripes

6. Grey Vertical stripes

Don't you worry, Rimmington family, I'm the world's best portrait painter! I can guarantee that this painting will be perfect to the very last detail!

This is no good at all! I can see 10 mistakes. You have made my whole family feel very sad!

Yes, we all feel sad.

Oh, dear! I feel very sad too!

Can you spot all 10 mistakes?

THE GIANT
KNIGHT
& THE GOLD THIEF

In a land full of brave and fearless heroes, the Giant Knight is the tallest of them all. He strides across the land in search of any clues that will help him solve a series of gold thefts that have occurred in the surrounding kingdoms.

Suddenly, among the greetings and cheers being shouted from the castles, the Giant Knight hears a voice cry for help. He springs into action and heads straight for the troubled tower. Well, as soon as he figures out where the shout for help is coming from, that is! Can you tell which castle is in trouble?

When he arrives at the castle, the Giant Knight finds Lord Dood in a tizzy. All of his gold has just been stolen!

It has only just happened, so the thief can't have gone far! My guards are searching the woods for him now. Can you help us find him? He has bunny ears, is wearing stripes, and is carrying a big sack with a star on it.

Can you see the gold thief?

THE GOLD THIEF
WAS HERE

The gold thief has disappeared again. Can you work out which way he
went by following his footprints?

There he is! The Giant Knight catches sight of the thief on the opposite side of an old bridge.

The Giant Knight must be careful when crossing the bridge though. There are a lot of cracks and he is heavy. Can you see a path that avoids the cracks?

The Giant Knight has almost caught up with the thief when he spots him escaping through a small cave entrance into a series of underground tunnels.

There's no way that the Giant Knight can follow the thief through the small tunnels, but luckily he's carrying his bag full of special items and super-helpful friends.

Somewhere in his backpack, among all the special items and super-helpful friends, is the Giant Knight's specially trained tracker dog. The tracker dog will be able to sniff out the gold thief wherever he is. All the Giant Knight needs to do is find the tracker dog in his bag and let it loose into the caves. Can you help him find it? (Hint: He has a big nose to sniff with, and he likes to wear stripes.)

The Giant Knight releases his tracker dog into the cave entrance, safe in the knowledge that wherever the gold thief is going, the dog will certainly find him.

All of a sudden, the Giant Knight hears barking in the distance. The tracker dog has caught up with the gold thief as he emerges on to a high cliff ledge. The Giant Knight spots them just in time to see the gold thief run right off the edge of the ledge!

However, instead of plummeting to the ground, the thief lands on a passing pterodactyl! He must have left it ready to help his escape! The gold thief shoots off into the sky, way out of reach of even the Giant knight!

The Giant Knight isn't about to give up the chase though, and he knows exactly what to do. He grabs a magic flute from his bag and plays one of the many magic songs that he knows. Summoned by the song, one of the Giant Knight's magic friends appears. Can you see who it is?

Thanks to his friend the flying whale, the Giant Knight can zoom up in to the sky and continue on his quest to capture the gold thief!

The Giant Knight spots the gold thief flying towards a distant cloud. Quick, Giant Knight, towards that cloud!

As they give chase through the sky, a passing group of flying rabbit snakes come to greet them. It's very lucky to see a flying rabbit snake, so the Giant Knight is very happy to see them.

He also thinks that two of the flying rabbit snakes must be twins, since they have exactly the same markings. Can you spot the twins?

The Giant Knight leaps off the flying whale and lands on the cloud island. In the distance he can see a castle so big it makes the Giant Knight feel small. The Giant Knight is not used to feeling small! He's not scared though, and starts to make his way across the lightest parts of the cloud towards the castle. Can you see the way to go?

As he gets closer, the Giant Knight
sees that the door is slightly open.
Without hesitation he steps inside.
Who or what will he find inside?
(Turn over to find out!)

When he steps inside the castle the Giant Knight is met by the super-massive sight of the gold thief's boss, King Giant Giant!

King Giant Giant is not alone, however. Can you see who is there with him?

"Fe-fi-fo! I guess we've been caught out!" says King Giant Giant.

"I suppose I should at least explain why we've been stealing so much gold..."

King Giant Giant explains how he had found an abandoned baby dragon on a nearby cloud, and had decided to take it in and look after it.

It was nice to have a new friend, but the only problem was that the only thing the dragon would eat was gold! He wouldn't even nibble on a piece of silver.

Eventually, the dragon had eaten all King Giant Giant's gold, and so he decided to send his little rabbit friend out to get gold from the Kingdoms below. He knew they were being bad, but he couldn't watch the dragon starve.

The Giant Knight listened carefully to King Giant Giant's story, and he realized that he actually had the answer to this whole problem right inside his bag ... his magic goose!

The magic goose is magic because she lays eggs made of solid gold! So, as long as the magic goose stays with King Giant Giant and his dragon, they will never be short of gold!

The Giant Knight is happy to leave his magic goose with King Giant Giant as long as they agree to keep half the golden eggs for the dragon, while the little rabbit gives the other half to all the kingdoms they've stolen gold from to make amends.

"One last thing," says King Giant Giant. "What does the magic goose eat?"

"Well," says the Giant Knight, "The only things she can eat are diamonds. . ."

THE END

There are 10 diamonds hidden throughout the Puzzleland section. Why don't you help King Giant Giant find them?

The island towns of Hibbleton and Dobbleford have been declared twin towns because they are so similar in so many ways. They are exactly the same! Well, almost...

While they are remarkably similar, the two towns are not completely the same in every way.

Can you see 10 differences between the twin towns?

Gladys loves her cats. Little Oscar always likes to stay inside the house, but the other 5 cats; Grayson, Mr. Snufflekins, Socksy, Dibble and Sandy, prefer to play out in the garden. Gladys doesn't worry about them though, since she can check on them through the window. Can you see them all?

Jim is fishing with Rosie and Hugo. One of them caught a fish, but their lines have got tangled. Can you tell who has caught the fish?

The Very Merry Tree believes
the key to a very merry life is to
keep everything in balance. For the Very
Merry Tree, this means getting the leaves
growing on his left side and the leaves growing on his right side to
match up. Can you help the Very Merry Tree find the 10 places
he needs to grow a new leaf to make each side have
the same number of leaves? This would make the Very Merry Tree very merry, indeed.

All the other girls at school like riding horses, but Sally is not interested in horses. As far as Sally is concerned, she much prefers riding her pet crocodile!

All the children (and the teachers, too) are scared of the crocodile and its rows of very sharp teeth. Sally has never noticed her crocodile's teeth, and she can't see what the big deal is. Can you connect the dots to show Sally where her crocodile's teeth are?

Nobody really has anything to worry about anyway since Sally's crocodile is a vegetarian crocodile. Can you find an apple for it to eat?

Astro Pete, space adventurer extraordinaire, is a good friend of the Super-Secret Space Spy Squad and is one of the few people they trust with information about their secret bases. He is being guided towards their newest super-secret spy base by following one of their super-secret rockets, but he's got confused by the vapour trails of some other passing rockets.

Can you help Astro Pete figure out the right direction to go by following the super-secret rocket's vapour trail?

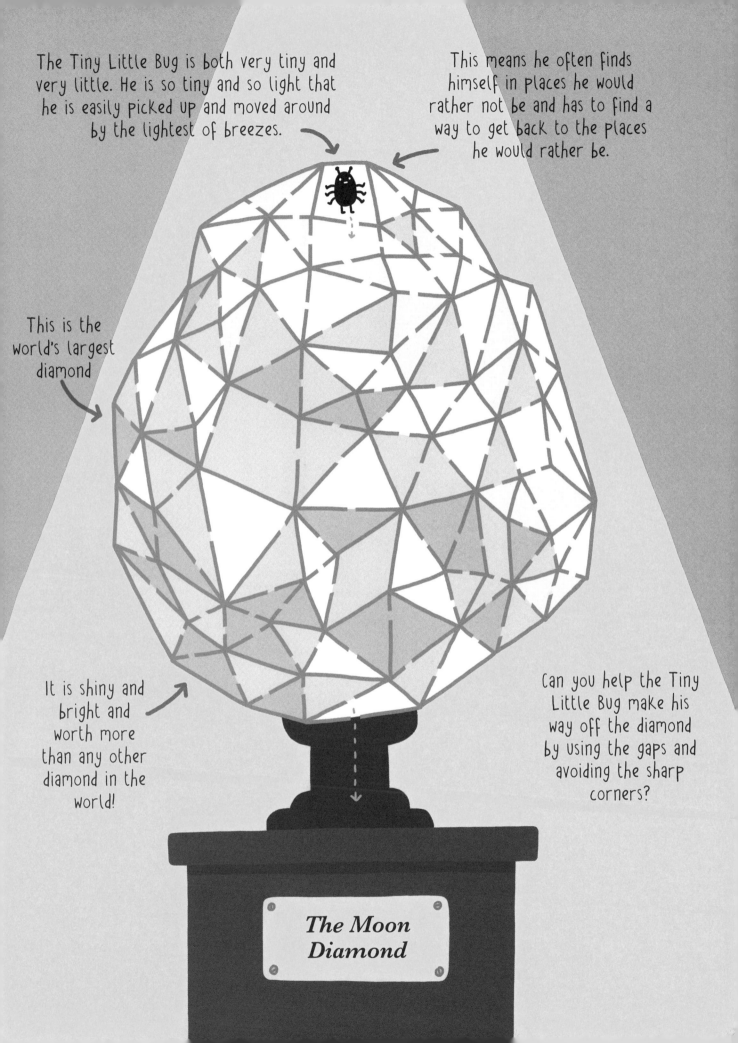

The Tiny Little Bug is both very tiny and very little. He is so tiny and so light that he is easily picked up and moved around by the lightest of breezes.

This means he often finds himself in places he would rather not be and has to find a way to get back to the places he would rather be.

This is the world's largest diamond

It is shiny and bright and worth more than any other diamond in the world!

Can you help the Tiny Little Bug make his way off the diamond by using the gaps and avoiding the sharp corners?

The Moon Diamond

Mr. Gnome is very careful about the security of his home. His front door has 10 locks, each with its own key. Sadly, Mr. Gnome is not very careful with his keys and has lost all 10 of them! Can you help him find them?

Rabbit always feels safe at night because his special friend in the moon watches over him. Can you see his friend?

Eddie has been kayaking all weekend. He is tired, wet and ready to get back home to the safety of the city. He has just enough time before plunging down one last waterfall to check which river will take him home. Be careful, Eddie! One wrong turn and you might get swept out to sea!

Mummy, the pattern on your dress is very pretty, but there is something wrong with your mirror...

I can see 15 differences between what your dress really looks like and how it looks in the mirror's reflection! Is it a magic mirror? I find it very confusing...

At last Jim has caught a fish! The only problem is he used a really old net with lots of gaps. The fish might be able to escape if it really wanted to (which it does!). Can you find the right way?

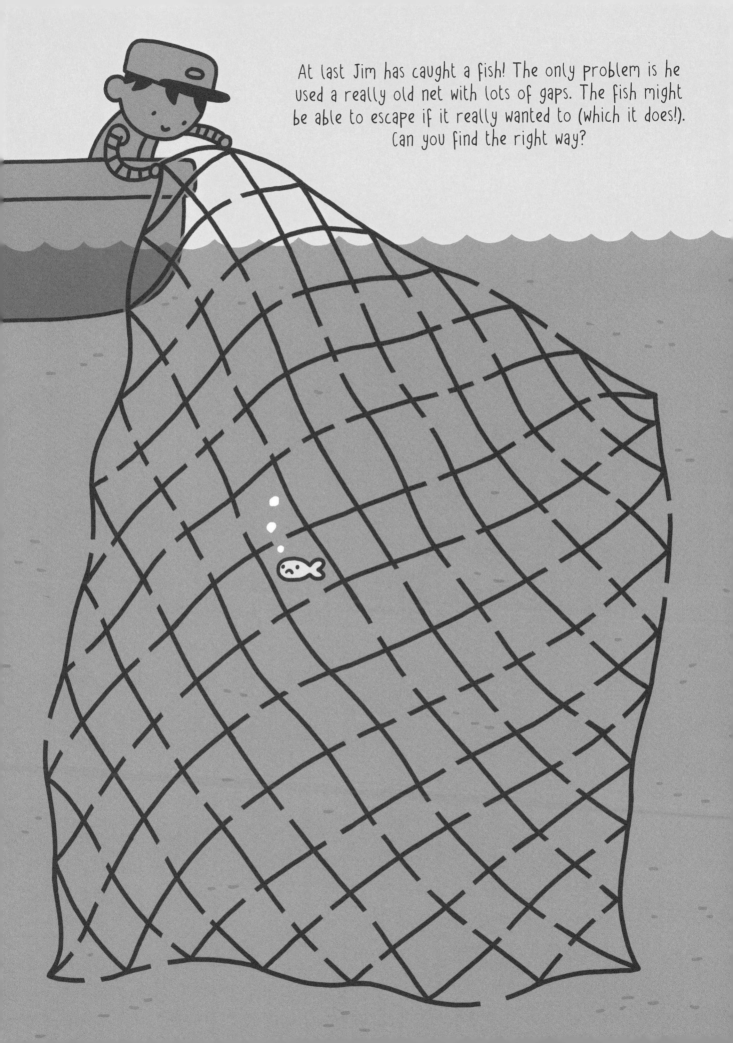

THE GAME MAKERS

This is Tim

This is Daisy

They work together at Superstar Games, the world's newest video game developer!

The Superstar Games company logo

They are about to start work on a brand-new game for a brand-new console named the Super Funston! They only have ten months before the Super Funston launches, so they need to get to work super fast!

The Super Funston video game console!

Daisy is designing the game's main character. They have decided that it will be called Rabbit Boy.

Why don't you help Daisy draw Rabbit Boy as he will appear in the game?

Tim is busy designing levels for the game. He has already started to mark out one of the levels on a grid, putting dots where the walls of the maze will be.

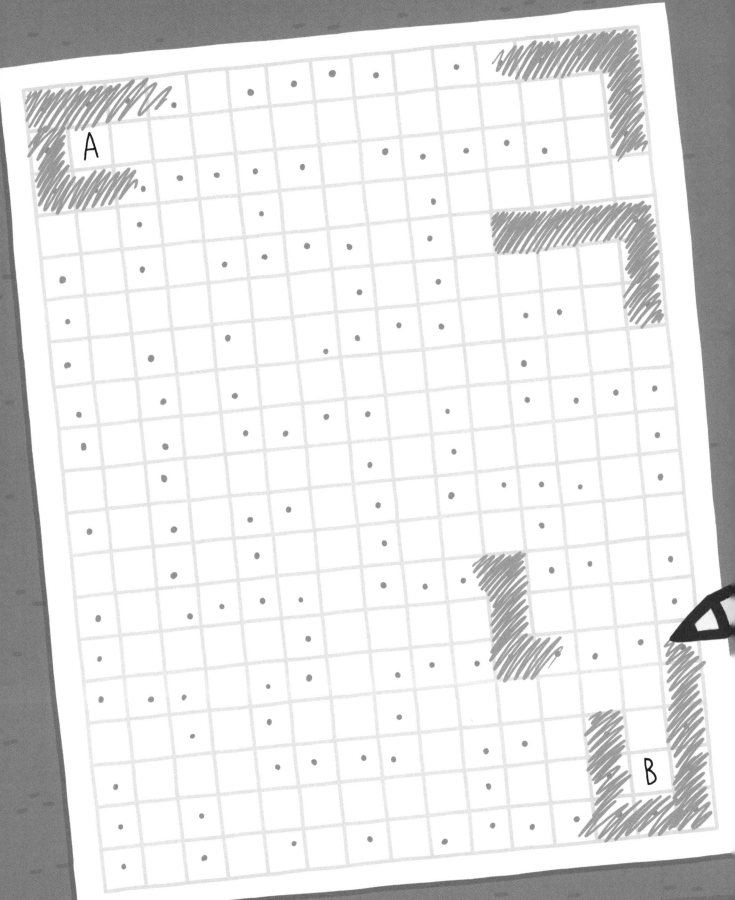

Tim was busy programming the game when suddenly it stopped working! When he looked at the programming code it was full of bugs and errors. He needs to go through the code to find every 'BUG' and every 'ERROR' and delete them. There are 5 of each hidden in the code. Can you help him find all 10 problems?

```
E G P R O C E S S B X E
R S B X B U G T F I G R
L Y U R U E W A O N T R
U N Z R G B M X X A J O
G T B X R E R R O R R R
E A U S H P R N E Y E E
R X G V A S E R V O R E
R A S C R C A D R B A S
O E R R O R D I G U B B
R K Q O E R R O R G D W
T B U G L S S U N I O H
F B Y B B O O T X D R O
```

Daisy is painting the artwork to go on the game's box.

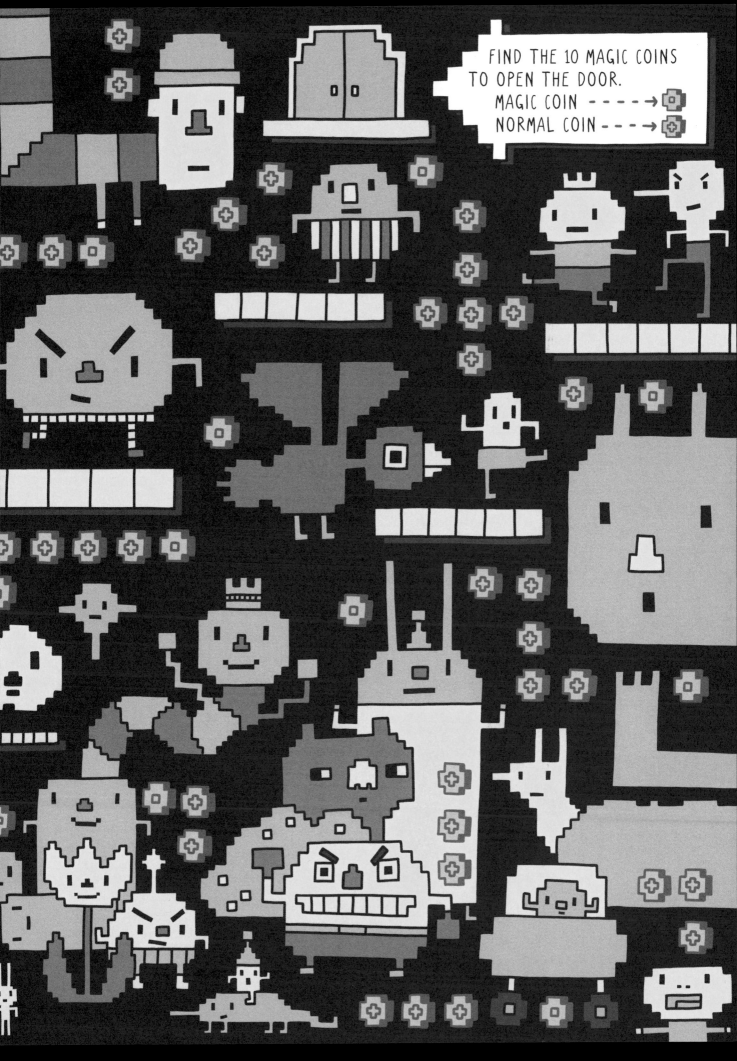

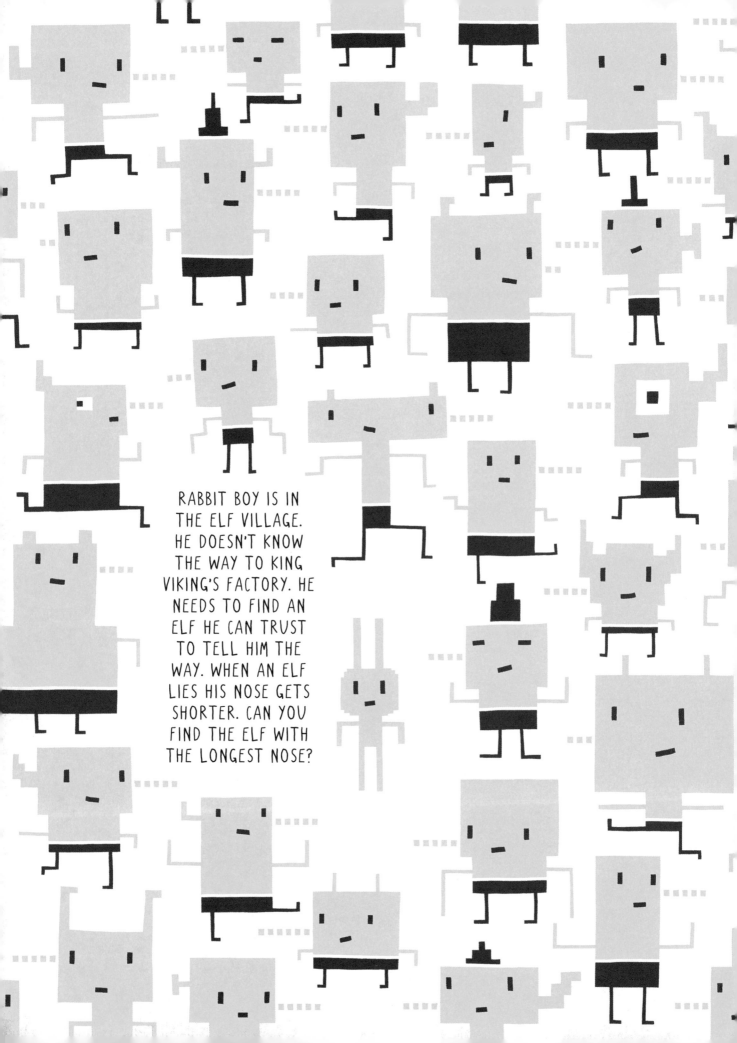

RABBIT BOY IS IN THE ELF VILLAGE. HE DOESN'T KNOW THE WAY TO KING VIKING'S FACTORY. HE NEEDS TO FIND AN ELF HE CAN TRUST TO TELL HIM THE WAY. WHEN AN ELF LIES HIS NOSE GETS SHORTER. CAN YOU FIND THE ELF WITH THE LONGEST NOSE?

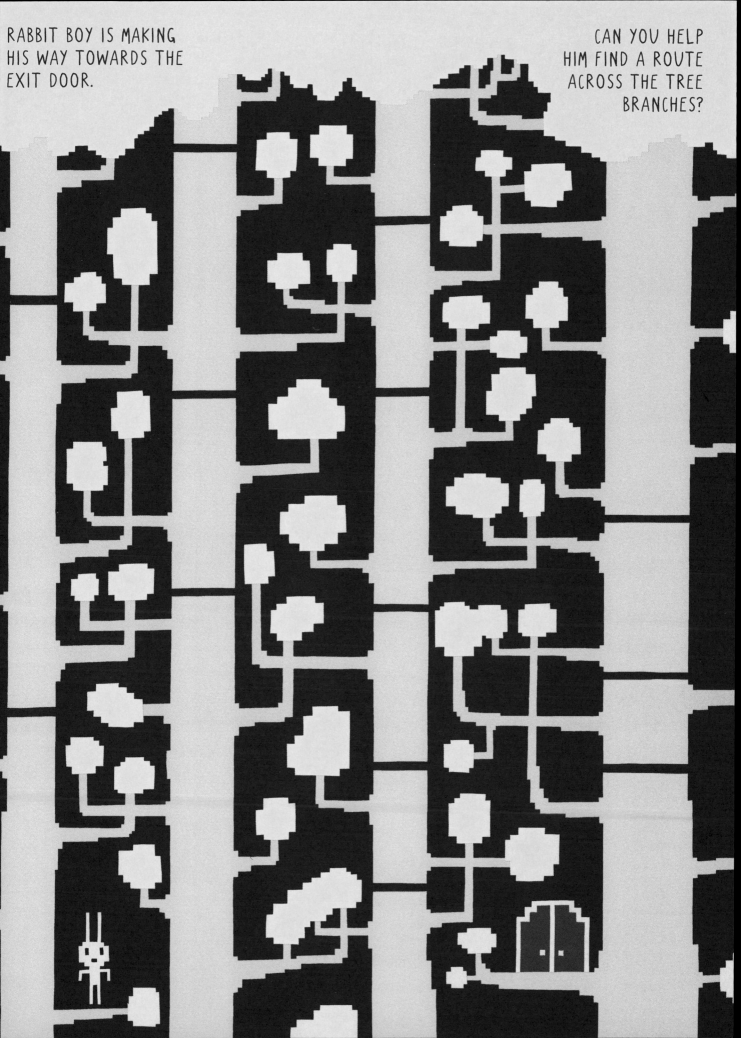

RABBIT BOY MUST FIND THE EXIT. BUT BEFORE THAT, HE NEEDS TO FIND THE KEY THAT WILL OPEN IT. WHICH PIPES WILL LEAD HIM TO THE KEY AND THE EXIT DOOR? WATCH OUT FOR PIPES THAT LEAD TO MONSTERS!

RABBIT BOY IS NEARLY AT KING VIKING'S FACTORY! THE ONLY PROBLEM IS THAT KING VIKING HAS TWO FACTORIES!

RABBIT BOY DECIDES THAT KING VIKING MUST BE INSIDE THE FACTORY THAT HAS THE MOST ROBOT GUARDS. WHICH ONE IS THAT?

RABBIT BOY IS IN KING VIKING'S FACTORY AT LAST. CLIMB THOSE LADDERS, RABBIT BOY, AND GET TO HIS LAIR!

IT'S KING VIKING IN HIS SUPER ROBOT!
THE END BOSS!
HA! HA! HA! RABBIT BOY, YOU WILL NEVER FIND MY SUPER ROBOT'S 10 WEAK POINTS AND YOU'LL NEVER GET YOUR SINGING DOG BACK! HE'LL HAVE TO SING FOR ME INSTEAD!

LUCKILY, RABBIT
BOY KNOWS
EXACTLY WHAT
THE SUPER
ROBOT'S WEAK
POINTS LOOK LIKE.
CAN YOU HELP HIM
FIND ALL 10? BE
QUICK AND HELP
SAVE SINGING DOG!

SINGING DOG HAS A
SPECIAL THANK-YOU
TREAT FOR RABBIT
BOY. CAN YOU SEE
WHAT IT IS?

GAME OVER!

THANK YOU FOR PLAYING!

The game is finished and is a great success! It has been at number 1 in the game charts for 10 weeks when Tim and Daisy get invited to the annual Video Game Awards!

Tim and Daisy are rewarded with a prize. Can you see what they won?

THE END

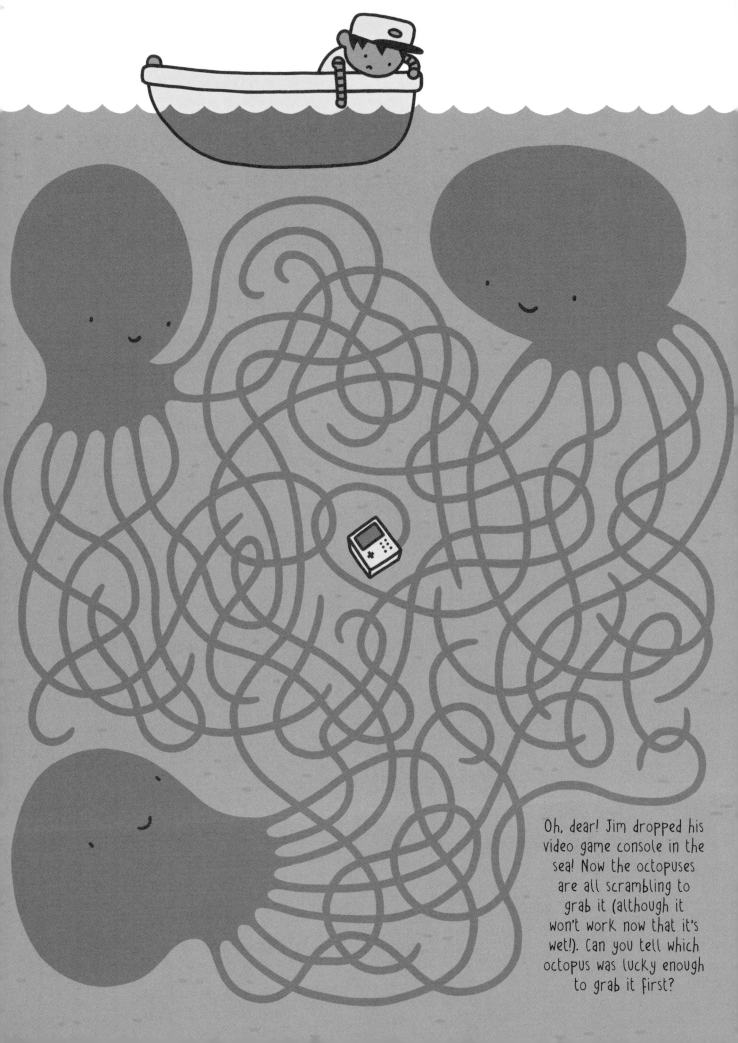

Oh, dear! Jim dropped his video game console in the sea! Now the octopuses are all scrambling to grab it (although it won't work now that it's wet!). Can you tell which octopus was lucky enough to grab it first?

I'm always feeling cold, but I look silly all wrapped up on hot, sunny days. I thought I'd found the answer; an invisible cloak! It could keep me warm and nobody would know I was wearing it!

I ordered one straightaway, but they have sent me this invisibility cloak instead! I'm warm, but I look like a ghost!

13
14
12
15
11
16
10
17
9
8
18
19
7
20
6
4
2
27
25
21
5
23
3
1
28
26
24
22

I really like dinosaurs, so I painted this picture of some! I spent weeks reading all the books I could find to make my painting as accurate as possible. I'm sure that there are no mistakes. I'm positive that every single detail is correct and perfect in every way. My painting shows the land of the dinosaurs exactly as it was. If someone found a way of going back in time to take a photo of what these dinosaurs looked like I'm sure they would look exactly like my painting. So there!

HELLO! I AM A TIME-TRAVELLING CAMERA-BOT. I GO BACK AND FORTH IN TIME TAKING PICTURES OF THE PAST AND THE FUTURE. LOOK AT THIS PICTURE I TOOK OF SOME DINOSAURS IN PREHISTORIC TIMES. DON'T THEY LOOK GREAT? MY PHOTO FINALLY SHOWS US EXACTLY WHAT DINOSAURS LOOKED LIKE.

Bad robot! Your photo made my painting look silly because of 10 mistakes I made. Sob!

OH YES. CAN YOU SEE THE 10 MISTAKES?

The spider was lucky that he managed to hide in a flower pot during the rain. He wants to get back to his web under the table before the rain starts again. He better be careful to avoid all of the puddles.

Miss Mottram and Class 2-B are looking very smart. They are all on their very best behaviour for their class photo.

There are actually two members of royalty in Class 2-B, Prince Richard and Princess Lucy! Can you spot them?

What's your favourite star constellation? I like the waving teddy bear. It's so cute!

I prefer the roaring
T. rex. It's awesome!

Paul has five pieces of this jigsaw left, but he only needs one. Which one piece will fill the gap?

After an unsuccessful day of fishing, Jim is returning back to land. As he thinks about where to buy his dinner, he notices something wrong with the town's reflection in the water. Can you spot the 10 differences that Jim has found?

Scholastic Children's Books,
Euston House, 24 Eversholt Street,
London NW1 1DB, UK

A division of Scholastic Ltd
London ~ New York ~ Toronto ~ Sydney ~ Auckland
Mexico City ~ New Delhi ~ Hong Kong

Originally published as Thomas Flintham's Marvellous Mazes (2011) and Thomas Flintham's Super-Fantastic
Puzzles (2012)

Text and illustrations © Thomas Flintham, 2011 and 2012.

ISBN 978 1407 15967 6

Printed and bound by Tien Wah Press Pte. Ltd, Malaysia

2 4 6 8 10 9 7 5 3 1